RETURN TO CHRISTIANITY

Return to Christianity

By

NELS F. S. FERRÉ

Abbot Professor of Christian Theology
Andover Newton Theological School

Publishers

HARPER & BROTHERS

NEW YORK and LONDON

RETURN TO CHRISTIANITY

FOURTH EDITION

H-U

Contents

Foreword

"Tho' truths in manhood darkly join,
Deep-seated in our mystic frame,
We yield all blessing to the name
Of Him that made them current coin."

IN THESE DAYS WHEN EARNEST SOULS LOOK FOR THE STAR of hope beyond the clouds of black despair we need the telescope of a clear redemptive word. Love is not enough. Even Christian love is not enough. Love in our common tongue is a word mixed, confused, sentimental, often erotic and debased.

Can that radical love that the first Christians realized in Christ, the love that became dynamic in the baptism of the Holy Spirit, be reborn in our hearts today? This love that in the "higher love endures" is the New Testament *agape*. It is the word by which the community of the redemptive fellowship christened itself when the living Church was born. It is the telescopic word by which to see our hope restored. All blessing to anyone who for our generation can make it current coin.

In *agape*, redemptive love, "now are we the sons of God and it doth not yet appear what we shall be, but we know that when He shall appear we shall be like Him for we shall see Him as He is; and every man that hath this hope in Him purifieth himself even as He is pure."

EVERETT C. HERRICK

Preface

THIS IS A DAY FOR DIRECT THINKING AND FOR STRAIGHT speaking. That fact was uppermost in my mind when I was asked to lecture on these four crucial topics of our day. It is a day when we must know what we believe, why we believe it, what we are going to do about it—and then dare to stand up and be counted. If parts of the book are strong medicine, the reason is that nothing less will cure our present illness. I have tried, as simply, candidly, and significantly as possible, to confront ourselves and our modern world with the radical Christian faith. We simply cannot be adequate for our day without being rooted and grounded.

That this little book is also my first general application of the Christian faith to our social problems need not be stressed, because it is altogether obvious that the treatment is sketchy and inadequate. But often a direct, unqualified treatment may be more satisfactory to the general reader than a long, complicated discussion. Those who see the implications of the Christian faith must surely affirm the need for drastic social reform and renewal. The whole question of social patterns raised in the last chapter is of especial importance.

The book may stir up controversy. It is not meant to do so. With all my heart and mind I hope that we can all leave behind the old controversies and in the light of the fuller Christian truth march straight forward to a reformed Church and a better social order. If the book will contribute to this end I shall indeed be deeply satisfied.

President Herrick, to whom the book is dedicated, is a close personal friend. He has read the manuscript and offered many helpful suggestions. Since I have not fully complied with his kindly but direct criticism where we did not see entirely eye to eye, I want to stress that he is in no way responsible for the ideas expressed in the book. His Foreword will mean much to all who know him.

I am indebted to Rev. J. Burt Bouwman, Executive Secretary, Michigan Council of Churches and Christian Education, under whose auspices the Conference was held; to Dr. W. H. Marbach, Chairman of the Conference; to Professor Charles A. Fisher, Director of the Extension Service of the University of Michigan, under the joint auspices of which the Conference was held and which made available the unusually attractive facilities of the University; to Professor Edward Blakeman, the official host of the University. The Conference is a really encouraging occurrence in the religious life of the country.

I am also grateful to the editors of Harper & Brothers, both for their help in publishing and for their personal friendship. Mr. David Scott first suggested my publishing a book for the general reader.

My wife, as always, has been with me through every stage of the preparation and publishing of the book. Her companionship, advice, and secretarial competence are the greatest help I have in my work.

NELS F. S. FERRÉ

Newton Centre, Mass.

RETURN TO CHRISTIANITY

1. Christianity and Truth

TEACH A RAT TO EXPECT PUNISHMENT WHENEVER A certain bell rings and reward whenever a different bell rings; then ring both bells together. The rat will show confusion, timidity, and indecision. In much the same way Christians today, confused by the ringing of many bells, are filled with indecision and a timid spirit. Today's greatest tragedy is not that the world, frustrated in its belief in a "century of progress," is in a mean and fearful mood while it watches and fans the holocaust. The greatest tragedy is not that masses suffering from the social patterns which make conflict natural find less and less help in what seems the drug dream of Christian faith. The greatest tragedy is not even that masses both inside and outside the churches, knowing full well their divisions, their thinness of faith, their confusion, their practical helplessness, and their continual subservience to the world, may here as elsewhere start a stampede away from a decaying religion to find what shelter they can in the vital modern "religions" of nation and race, of violence and material goods. The greatest tragedy is, far rather, that Christian leaders who are supposed to offer the world help and guidance themselves stand confused, timid, and powerless.

Unless we can concretely prove in both faith and life that Christianity offers the way and the power to a new and better order of life, the idealism and the cynicism of our age may well join forces to destroy the "Christian" institution for the sake of taking some well-marked short cut to the promised land. Our age is a seeking age. It has fairly stopped to look and listen. However skeptical it may seem, therefore, and however much of its idealism may run outside organized "Christianity," this age would once again hearken to a clear and sound Christian bell because it knows all too well that its own bell is cracked. It would surely pay more heed to the church bells if they, too, were not cracked. Our task is to melt down these cracked bells and to forge a Christian bell that will ring true enough to be convincing and loud enough to be heard. To be listened to, Christianity must offer both a convicting analysis of its own and of the world's troubles and a genuine demonstration of its truth to find, and power to effect, the new world.

The word "Christian" has largely lost its true meaning. We talk about the "Christian" this and the "Christian" that. But actually both this and that are obviously far from Christian. The use is both illegitimate and destructive. Naturally it has a practical purpose and historic and sociological truth, and can even find some religious justification. But the very use of it denies the Christian claim as to its own nature. To assist in understanding clearly our modern situation, we shall use quotation marks with the confused, divided, rather impotent medley of organizations, doctrines, and customs called Christian and reserve the full term for its true use. This we shall define before the end of the chapter. The many questions that come to mind with regard to this distinction will be answered throughout the entire discussion of the book.

The bell to which this age has listened most intently is science. And with good reason. Science has revolutionized the world not only by making it richer and more comfortable but also by forging a new and sharper weapon of truth to slay a number of giants of despair which thrived on the myths of history and religion. To say that the practical success of science alone accounts for its method having been taken over as far as possible into all fields of learning, therefore, is absurdly unfair. He who cares for humanity and for truth must feel a real sense of gratitude for the exceedingly valuable contributions of science in practically all areas of life. In a peculiar way science is the unique and distinguished achievement of the modern world. Damp and cold to the highest human hopes though the world view of science may have been, man must know the truth and live by it. Besides, man adjusts himself so amazingly, even to an ultimate and eventual emptiness, that even in this thin soil, most inhospitable to religion, there began to grow a delicate but beautiful flower of the human spirit, as ardent souls have wrung from the vast darkness some flickering hope and fugitive meaning. If life is but a wave there is beauty in its breaking; there is a portion of enjoyment within the transient tragedy of life; the heartache of tomorrow's world can be a trifle eased by today's curative efforts; and the limitless unconscious cannot oppress the gasp of spirit that is no more. For the human spirit even oppressive knowledge, provided it is definite, is better than uncertainty and confusion.

But now this bell, too, has cracked. Science has nothing to say, at least directly, about the ultimate nature of reality. It only describes our physical-historical world. This has long been clear to many, but now scientists and educators in increasing numbers are beginning to share this basic understanding. Technically speaking, with respect to the principles of ultimate truth, science is positivistic; that is, as strict science rather than as quack philosophy, it never presumes to say what is the nature of the really real. By not being scientific enough, men have turned a limited method into a limitless dogma; they now begin to understand that the equation of scientific method with a naturalistic metaphysics is not in itself scientific.

The leap from a neat but limited method to the assumption that science contains and explains all the truth that can be known, while altogether natural, is none the less a leap far beyond the proper efficacy and scope of the scientific method itself that is falsely destructive of man's faith in the saving reality of the most high. The question today is no longer so much between faith and fact as between the kinds of fact that have the unconditional right to compel our faith. The limits of science as a theory of truth have now been drawn; and, therefore, open and vital modern minds are ready to seek new means with which to fashion our intellectual material into solid foundations for both individual and social faith. Our biggest problem at this point is that general education has so long trained our youth in the catechism of science that its indoctrinated faith in science as all the truth there is has become an unconscious axiom. But just as what yesterday's leaders ignorantly taught is today's popular atmosphere, so what today's leaders think can become tomorrow's hospitable climate for a more constructive faith.

As a self-sufficient way to truth and the good life, moreover, science has failed man not only theoretically but also practically. It was man's hope that more scientific knowledge and greater technological progress would necessarily mean a new day of human brotherhood. With the gradual elimination of material want, man would surely become his true and reasonable self, living henceforth forever in the increasing co-operation of light and life. He found instead that the tools in his hands could be used by demons to destroy his material achievement, to let loose floods of hate and division, and to turn him back toward the moral jungle. Never was civilization so broadly and deeply threatened as in the brightest day of scientific achievement. Never have men had the chance to see so clearly that *apart from moral purpose* reason can be prostituted for the lowest ends.

Mere knowledge will give neither high purpose nor moral drive. Man, the living being, is not the neutral scientist but is driven by conflicting passions which, unless they are lifted and led, will tear and wreck instead of heal and build. As a self-sufficient savior, therefore, science has failed even practically; and more and more, in the depths of their consciousness, men are awakening to this fact. Under the stress of critical decisions and of the moral weariness of the times, an increasing number of men, from national collegiate societies to news correspondents, from the man on the street to the learned educator, are acknowledging the need to unchain reason from a narrow scientific method within the realms of truth and value, in order to find the light and the transforming power of Christian ideals, or, at least, of those everlasting realities which condition and control our lives. Yet many keep clinging almost desperately to science as the sovereign way to truth because no one has been able to tell them convincingly, "Behold, I show you a more excellent way." Is there, then, some more significant way to truth?

If we turn to "Christianity," furthermore, what do we find? We find two main branches: the traditional and the modernist. Both of these, like science, have failed man both theoretically and practically. Christianity claims that God is self-giving love and that He made the world that men might have an organic fellowship based on trust in Him and issuing in a creative and responsible concern by all and each for each and all. This God, Christianity claims, is the sole source of creation, at once all-powerful, all-wise, and all-good. This claim that God as *agape*, or unlimited, objective, self-giving love, is central for both faith and life constitutes the fulfilling and revolutionary uniqueness of Christian faith, which should dominate its very last and least doctrine. In this Christian ideal, too, modern man believes to a surprising extent; but when he looks at traditional theology, what does he find?

He finds not only that it is inconsistent in theory, but also that it actually denies its central affirmation at crucial points of both faith and life. He finds, in fact, a dogmatic system which talks about a personal devil who will actually possess most men in an eternal hell which itself depends for its very existence upon the being and activity of God. He finds a little Ptolemaic God of human history and, even worse, a little scheme which does not usually bother to justify God's relation with all people, all lives, and all conditions of men at all times and in all places in terms of a strict but compassionate Father's love. He finds a spirit that has fought for every obscurantism and literalism, against the best men of science who dared to suffer for the truth, a spirit which even to this day fights against rather than for the facts when they challenge the miniature dimensions of its Lilliputian theology. Altogether too often he finds revolting ideas which in their utter crudeness rival the immoral myths of primitive religions. He finds also every ingenious kind of rationalization to defend dogmas which ought to have been either buried, to release in new growth the dried kernel of life, or at least winnowed from the mass of chaff.

Modern man cannot force his spirit into the strait jacket of such a repulsive religion. Only those who have never fully opened their eyes to the light of the fuller truth can live with deep conviction within the inconsistencies of traditional theology. These have usually an enviable zeal for the Lord, but alas, a zeal not according to knowledge. Many traditionalists, too, are bigger than their doctrines, or hold dead doctrines. They are true to the whole dogma because they possess no adequate principle of discrimination by which to discard the false and release the true. The highest peak of revelation given to man—that God is love and light and that in Him there is no darkness at all—traditional theology has, in any case, hidden in the hazy mists of dogma and the low-hanging clouds of mythology. Instead of developing a theology definitely in line with God's full truth in Christ, it developed a dogmatic crust, conserving the proportion of good and bad within the actual, perhaps in order unconsciously to ward off the true Christian faith and its radical implications for all the realms of human conduct. It seems almost as though the Holy Spirit *had* to develop science, history, and rational philosophy (and that mostly outside the church) in order to crack this crust of traditional theology and set free the great truth of Christianity. God was surely good to the world when He unleashed science and history to break as twigs all the infantile attitudes of actual Christianity and to knock from under it the puny staff of literalism on which it leaned. Theoretically, traditional theology has failed, and modern man cannot return to it except he succumb to the destructive fear of some tragic regression to moral childhood.

Traditional theology failed because, instead of believing in the power of God's love (as shown in the life, teachings, and death of Jesus Christ) to transform both man and society, it merely projected actuality as it now is, with its good and bad, into an intensified eternal dimension—giving the devil more than his due, at that—and then froze it all into perpetuity. In this way it denied conclusively that God as love is the ultimate principle of explanation. Because it did not feel the claim and power of God's love, vividly and concretely, on all human relations, traditional theology similarly failed in the practical realm, for there it lowered its demand on conduct, particularly on that of society, almost to the point of the prevailing conventional standards. Because it worshiped God the defeated Creator, traditional theology could not believe that the Gospel applied in a revolutionary way to all human relations. Christendom, having thus given up the true Christian faith, and enervated by its faith in a god made nearly as powerless as its own image, has now all too often taken to calling Christian realism that pessimism which denies the full power of the Gospel. Just as traditional theology, therefore, made impossible its highest peak of faith, so it also leveled off the highest peak of Christian practice.

Though there have been exceptions, the Church in general sank so low as to sanction almost every form of social evil: for instance, to sanction war—every war, everywhere, and on all sides where Christians were involved—even to the point of sending out armies of little children, carrying consecrated crosses along with the sword; to defend *laissez-faire* capitalism in the name of religious freedom; to uphold race oppression in the name of social order; to withstand science and education; and in general to harbor and abet all kinds of reactionism. Christian faith, it sometimes seems, was taken over by mankind as a rationalization with which it could identify itself in order never to see its actual self. Mostly by God's good grace, we can now see, "Christianity" as the opium of the people was swept out of Russia; but even in today's America, in this admittedly unholy conflict, historic church bells are being melted down for ammunition—calling in question, at least, the extent to which these bells have ever been summoning men to the God of Jesus Christ.

Just as eternal truth, however, could not be confined within the dogmatic crust of traditional theology, but seeped out with capillary strength to make for science, history, and a more moral conscience that later cracked the crust; so in the same way the compromised social conduct within the old wineskins contained the true wine of the spirit' which is now beginning to break them asunder. The spirit is now beginning to be seen more and more in its full strength; and for its embodiment on earth as it is in heaven, there begins to be increasing clamor.

Naturally we are not speaking against traditions as such. We appreciate them. Apart from them religions cannot live. They are the calyx that supports and protects the flower. How can the flower spring directly from the root? We can never do without the calyx in Christian growth. The traditions are the skin of the Christian fruit, the bark of its tree. History has no ideals floating around loose without degrees of embodiment. And that involves the perversion and the partial failure of the ideals. But if they are rooted in reality and truth, some degree of success is likely to characterize their lives; unless, of course, they are born entirely out of their time. Whitehead says that a great idea takes a thousand years and sometimes much more to mature in history and to reach the general consciousness even as a relevant ideal. The great new truth may break into history with sudden power and then either lie fairly dormant or spread but slowly and partially. However inadequate institutions and traditions may be, they preserve and nourish the truth which gave them birth—unless they so pervert it as to obscure it and render it ineffective. This is the value and the danger of traditions.

We are grateful for our traditions for they have kept alive in history the great Christian truth. Our traditions are the deep roots that have contained the Christian life that has burrowed deeper and deeper into the historic consciousness of our world. Modern man has often forgotten the roots, been unappreciative of the traditions, and looked to some superficial modernity to solve his deep historic problems. History never works that way. In that direction lies superficiality, disillusion, and despair. That which can give strong new growth must have deep roots. In dreary weather the roots may grow the best and the plants become the strongest. The Christian roots have been growing for a long time. They are deep. But the plant has been badly cared for. Its nature and needs have not been adequately understood. The old traditions must be reinterpreted in the light and strength of the real life of Christianity. They have obscured the real Christian truth altogether too much. They have made true Christianity unreal and repulsive to great masses of thoughtful people, and the young are badly confused and indifferent. The writer has tried in a previous book[1] to show how deep and true the Christian doctrines are when they are understood in the full light of the essence of Christianity. We can keep the strength of the old and deep roots and yet prepare the plant for vigorous new growth. We need many to work hard and long on the task. There is everywhere a hunger for that which springs from deep roots, pruned and cleansed for fresh new growth. As any chicken farmer knows, you can get quick green growth, high and lush, by warming a breadpan of soaked oats in the oven at the right temperature. We dread such growth for it has no lasting roots. We have drawn the lines of our present analysis with rigorous sharpness to bring out the points clearly, for we must release the life of the deep roots and prepare for the needed growth of a new day.

Science failed to give man significant spiritual truth and to provide the moral dynamics to achieve it; traditional theology failed to give man a high enough truth and one that could by its very nature challenge and transform all of life. Modernism, too,

[1] *The Christian Faith.*

has failed both theoretically and practically. Theoretically modernism failed because its standards were not primarily religious. It, too, harbored an inconsistency within its thought. It claimed to be a religion, i.e., a faith, but its standards were those of science and reason operating within the limits of what can be demonstrably seen and known. Why modernism should have chosen these standards is, of course, easy to understand, for these were the borrowed tools with which it had cracked the crust of traditional theology.

Here, then, was the basic inconsistency within modernism: While science and reason deal competently only within the created realm, the center of Christian faith is always beyond what is here and now actual, and can therefore never be proved in its terms. There is no question at all about the necessity of using our minds at all times as critically and carefully as well as creatively and adequately as possible. All ought to agree to the most vigorous and accurate use of mind and to the fullest possible honesty in the pursuit of truth. The real point, however, is that the God and Father of our Lord Jesus Christ, the Creator of the ends of the earth and of the immeasurable realms beyond the earth, can never be reduced to the *kind* of proof open to any science or philosophy that claims controlled conditions and adequate verification. He must be met, accepted, and understood in vision and power.

If the ideal which is far greater and more real than the actual can be proved in *its* terms (beyond, of course, that it is relevant to it, organically applicable to it, and has the power to transform it), it is precisely by this very fact not the ideal of high faith. Religion lives by faith. The life of high religion is trust in what in its fullness is beyond human control and understanding. Modernism was caught in this dilemma of its own inconsistency: Either it reduced its content increasingly to what could be proved, and therefore became less and less an adequate faith; or else it kept "preaching its hopes" with an increasing realization that in the light of its own standards it was to a large degree an arbitrary assumption. Modernism failed to understand that religion has its own standards, its own perspectives, its own sources of assurance. God's spirit can never be reduced or wholly proved in terms of His created works, especially as obscured by the demonic elements of historic process. God can be known concretely only to a faith that sees and feels beyond present attainment. All the hosts of confirmatory reasons for believing in Christianity are, therefore, of but secondary, though vital, importance. The standard of Christian faith, however, is its highest revelation, a transcendent God of love who is both the Most High and the Most Real.

Modernism as a religious faith not only becomes thin or without solid intellectual foundations but also, because of its standards, tends to become overly intellectualistic. Faith appeals primarily to the will and the emotions. Therefore faith, though needing direction, has drive. Fearing the depths of life in feeling and decision, and finding its faith, in so far as it was full and rich, incapable of the kind and measure of verification it sought, modernism found itself increasingly torn by confusion and indecision and bored from within by skepticism and sophistication until it became afraid of driving passions. It dried up. It fed hungry souls on wartime rations as though Christianity were suffering from a steady siege. It was definitely on the defensive. Modernism lived, moreover, altogether too much on the religious power of those who had joined its forces in rebellion against traditional theology. It was negative in faith and positive only in protest. It lacked vitality.

The failure of modernism was due, in fact, to its low birth rate. It had direction but little drive; vision, but little power.

And its failure was due to its oppression by false standards which made the modernist apologetic about his faith except as a crusader against the backwardness of traditional mythology. His will to believe was choked by his doubt as to his right to believe. Because modernism did not dare to be primarily a religion, a vigorous faith, it was robbed of its dynamic power. While it lived on inherited spiritual capital, and drew on faith in practice more than in theory, it produced most desirable fruits; but all the while it kept hacking away even what roots it still had. Although its Christian sensitivity gave it social concern, it tended to lose both religious and social force because it was all the while blind to the fact that an adequate religion must have its source, standard, and dynamics in a power primarily not of this world. Modernism failed to move men deeply enough and widely enough, not because it was overly enlightened but because it was insufficiently religious.

We ought, perhaps, to sum up our analysis before we go on to suggest the nature of Christian truth. We have said that science as a self-sufficient way to truth failed theoretically because by the limitations inherent in its own method it tells us nothing final about the nature of ultimate truth; it failed practically because its new information and physical achievements must always be subject to a moral drive and direction which it could not provide. We found also that traditional theology failed theoretically because it was not consistent with Christianity's central affirmation that God is all-powerful and all-wise love, and because it reduced God's absolute scale of magnitude to its own infinitesimal drop of historic time. Traditional theology also failed practically because it became generally allied with the *status quo* in the world of politics, economics, and social customs, and was not a daring prophetic power for the transformation of all the relationships of men.

Modernism failed theoretically because it gave up the Christian faith itself as the primary standard of truth, accepting instead as primary the secondary standards of reason and experience in so far as these could demonstrate the truth of religion in terms of what is here and now actual; it failed practically as well because its inner intellectual inconsistency choked off its religious drive. Faith is power. The Christian faith, when central in thought and practice, can heal and transform all of life. This power modernism lacked. Thus while traditional theology was not Christian enough, modernism was not religious enough. Now, freed from the false claims of science, we must accept resolutely in thought and life the Christian faith which is God's power of salvation for both the individual and society.

Christianity must, in short, become radical. "Radical" comes from the Latin *radix*, meaning "root." Radical Christianity is simply root Christianity. Every great reform in Christianity has come from going back to the root. But the reforms have not been radical enough. Because of an understandable emotional conservativism, the reformers have all too often carried along secondary and conflicting dogmatic material. Radical Christianity resolutely makes the New Testament God of *agape,* i.e., of responsible self-giving concern, central in both faith and life. Radical Christianity is the critical revolution of faith and life to which the world must come before it can find itself. It alone, we believe, can fully satisfy man's deepest needs and solve his basic problems. God himself has made us for a new kind of community, based on *agape*, for which Jesus lived, taught, and died. This is a community, under God, of responsible, creative, self-giving concern. This is a fellowship functioning through the organic law by which each member of a body lives for the whole body and the whole body for each member—this law raised not just to the high, human, super-organic level of purposeful personal relations, but even to the divine level where it is sustained as well as initiated according to God's central purpose in creation and history.

Radical Christianity is the revolution that destroys evil at its roots, no matter how tangled, but even as it destroys brings fairer flowers of life and civilization. Radical Christianity may have to meet the cross within as well as without the churches the more it begins to sweep away the churches' false dogmatic alliances and to throw the money-changers out of the temple. But it offers the young all the idealism of which life is capable; it offers the mature all the wisdom that wields the scalpel on life in order to save life; it offers all a Christian faith that is both unreservedly Christian and deeply religious. Here is power; here is peace; here is salvation.

Three qualities at least must characterize radical Christianity. It must, first of all, be *resolutely and primarily a faith* (though a faith organically related to reason and experience). Its special revelation must be its primary authority. The revelation is special because it is the selective rather than the general disclosure in history of what God in Himself really is. The best, the least common, actual life, the *special* life, reveals God the most. Faith has its own validity. This is the basic claim of religion. Religious validity can never be reduced to some other kind of validity without violating its own nature, without surrendering its assurance, without forfeiting its authority, without losing its dynamics. The center and power of Christian faith is not of this world. Theology is not the same thing as philosophy. Theology deals with the content of religious truth in the light of its own perspective. This perspective is not primarily practical but is concerned above all with the fullest possible living truth, *a truth of which faith is the necessary means as the living decision whereby the most high becomes the most real.*

Yet faith without reason tends to become arbitrary and fanatical. Reason and experience must, therefore, check and challenge faith as to its adequacy. Faith must prove in the court of reasoned experience that it is relevant to all experience, practically applicable to all actual situations of life, and able to transform, radically and desirable, all of life and to save it from meaninglessness, evil, and destruction. Reasoned experience thus keeps faith from artificial dogma and arbitrary creed, but is yet, as authority, only a secondary standard. Adequate faith possesses in its own object its own irreplaceable and irreducible validity.

For Christian faith, Jesus is the clearest way to God, the mediator of God's fullest light and life, and the founder of the fellowship in which man finds his fullest salvation. This faith, therefore, is centered not alone in Jesus the historic figure but in the eternal reality and purposes of God Himself as made known and effective through him. We definitely do not teach merely an idea as the essence of the Christian faith. God and nothing less than God is the center of Christian faith. Yet even though the standard and dynamics of Christian faith is this special, fulfilling revelation, this must always, we repeat, be checked and challenged by reason with respect to its organic relation to general experience.

Unless we can know that Christian faith is increasingly adequate to human needs the more we know both it and them; unless it fulfills them, in however unexpected and immediately undesired ways, on a level of satisfaction more basic and organic than any other; unless it be thoroughly applicable to the whole man and men in all their relations; and unless it produce the power of truly desirable transformation and the dynamics of

salvation, Christian faith is not authoritative but arbitrary. When
all this is said, however, we must stress as even more necessary
for our day the truth that the ultimate reality and authority
of faith's object cannot be proved in terms of general experience;
and that Christianity, if it be man's most adequate faith, must
never again surrender its birthright as a religion to non-religious
standards. Religion has its own knowledge and power. It cannot stand straight and steady unless it learns to stand on its own
feet.[2]

In the second place, Christianity has its own way of knowing. A careful philosophic analysis would bring out that Christianity as a metaphysics can muster powerful theoretical con-
firmation along many lines. We accept with true gratitude all
that reason can give. No religion will live long and healthily
in the modern world without a sincere respect for all truth. The
honest heart craves an honest mind and the critical and candid
spirit. But the very nature of religious truth is such that seeing
can take place only according to the conditions inherent in
religious knowledge. All speculative lines of verification, sev-
erally and together, are but the courts of the gentiles and can
never reveal either the full knowledge or the full power of the
holy of holies. Live religion lives by worship, by prayer, by
fellowship, by obedience, by service, by personal vision, by
walking with God. Even in the realm of religious truth there
can be no substitute for personal religion.[3]

Without the understanding that religion is man's most important business, no one can truly see God. Christian knowledge
involves the continual surrender of our will to God's will.
The culminating truth of Christian faith comes not primarily

[2] For a more detailed discussion, cf. the author's article, "Faith and Reason," in *Christendom* Spring 1943.
[3] Cf. D. C. Macintosh's challenging book, *Personal Religion*.

through speculation in the study but through life with God in the light and power of Christ. Pure and humble prayer by a person with a single eye and a surrendered life is the only gate that leads up to the height of vision. The light of Christ becomes creedally dimmed unless it mediates to the man of faith the vision of God through the communion of the commonplace. Simple responsibilities humbly and faithfully accepted become metaphysical experiences. The knowledge of God may be most real to us as we give a cup of cold water in His name or carry close to our hearts a neighbor's sorrow. The light of God comes to those who are teachable in spirit and seek for Him where He is to be found. The sophisticated by their very sophistication hide themselves from God and their fellow men. The proud and the self-sufficient prefer their own darkness to the light of life. The self-seeking cannot know God for God is love and he that is not willing to love his brother is not willing to know the God who is love.

The light of the Christian God comes as we read the Scriptures, live with the saints, and try to picture our world as God would have it. If our hearts are first of all in the world, they see only the God of the shadows and cannot believe the God of the full light to be real. The knowledge of God is man's most precious possession and demands not only spiritual discipline but also spiritual surrender. All other knowledge stops short of vision. All other arguments, however many and searching, are but theory. Christian faith gives a deep assurance far beyond what we can see and control, but only as we humbly lean on God, let ourselves be lighted by His light, and lifted by His power. Religious vision to be real must first of all trust God enough to be itself. A healthy faith does not beg to be declared genuine.

We need a new theology organically combining faith and

reason, characterized by great intellectual rigor as well as vigor, and equipped with keen analysis and powerful insights along new and deeper lines. We need a religious knowledge that dares to see and know that the Lord is good and ever dependable. We need also, in the last place, a radical Christianity that so unmistakably shows the signs of the spirit, that is so vital, that has such insight, power, concern, wisdom, and victorious enthusiasm, that shows, in short, such adequacy of life and such authority of spirit that men will own the source because they cannot deny the effects. A world undone will surely turn to a fellowship of life which it sees beyond a doubt unites men organically and gives them power to desire, to sustain, and to achieve their greatest vision. If we truly show men the fruits of the spirit, will they not seek for themselves the spirit itself?

As Christendom becomes radically Christian in spirit and in truth, God will give us the Kingdom. That is His good pleasure. No political theory, no social change on the human level, no institutional reform can *by itself* give us a new order. Christianity is God's truth to man in the fullness of time; and only as God's will is accepted in heart and mind can we obtain that adequate, universal community which by its very inmost nature involves all the changes necessary to the social patterns of a saved society.

2. Christianity and the Individual

A NUMBER OF OUR BASIC PROBLEMS ARE CONCERNED WITH the relation of the individual to society. Christianity, if it is truth, must throw light on these problems. One reason for our conviction that Christianity *is* truth, therefore, is that, as far as we can see, it does offer adequate solution to the basic questions involved in the relation of the individual to society. These are chiefly three: (1) the conflict between the will to self and the need for fellowship; (2) the conflict between the will to spontaneity and variety and the need for unity and order; (3) the conflict between immediate concern and satisfaction and the need for ultimate meaning and sanction.

There is in every man, first of all, this struggle between the will to self and the need for fellowship. This is a fact. We shall get further in understanding both man and the Christian faith when we stop trying to prove that man is either radically good or radically bad. Those who declare him to be radically bad know the depth of man's conflict but fail to see it in the light of its total meaning; while those who declare him to be radically good may see more of the meaning of his conflict but miss its depth. The conflict between self and society may be more or less acute, but it exists in the saint as well as in the sinner. As far as we know, no one is completely concerned with the welfare of society and no one, normally and morally alive, is completely indifferent to all of society. There is no self that is not also a *socius*; there is no *socius* that is not also a self.

We shall not here attempt to elaborate this point or to document it. The appeal is to the primary evidence of each man's experience. Though we may be unequally aware of the struggle, we all have it. Even Jesus, on the one hand, knew the temptations in the wilderness and the inner agony of Gethsemane; and the cruelest or the most self-satisfied of men, on the other, feels the need to relate himself to society and to make some impression on it. We dare to go even so far as to suggest that every normal person wishes to be liked by at least someone, and perhaps even to be respected and appreciated. In any case, everyone wants to "belong" in some way, to have some function, or to relate himself to his kind if only in a world of the past or of the future, or in some imaginary world to which he has escaped. We may think of this in terms of the fact that the will to live is not naturally an entire will to love, and that the will to love is never wholly present in any person apart from some will to self. It simply is wrong, furthermore, to say that the will to self is easily realized in the will to love. There is, rather, a deep, continuing opposition between them.

On the one side is the natural self-centeredness which expresses itself in such terms as the instinct to self-preservation, the tendency to invidious comparison, the naturalness of self-esteem, the will to social recognition, the desire for self-sufficiency, the will to superiority, the hope for personal gain, and the will to power. We all know how close to us all are the self-centered vices of pride, possessiveness, and pretense. On the other side, however, is this need for fellowship which is so strong that even our vices have social reference and command some kind of social currency. The fact is clear that man is a social animal to the point where the self-calculating individual finds deep satisfaction neither with nor without society.

How does Christian love, or, to use the Greek word, *agape*, solve this problem? Christian *agape* is complete, self-giving concern for others. A community on the basis of Christian love creates individuals entirely concerned with the fellowship and a fellowship wholly concerned with each individual. In such a community all selfishness is gone; all indifference is gone; all the ignorance which springs from individual and social inertia and from the defensive rationalizations of weak or evil wills is also gone. In such a community all self-centered fear is banished since no one any longer lives first of all for himself. There is concern, but no defensive anxiety over the standing of the ego, or over any possible suppression or oppression of the self by the community. Perfect love does cast out fear. In it there is no suspicion, no envy, no evil imagination of the heart. The individual finds himself in a friendly, appreciative, helpful fellowship which brings out the best in him in terms of growth, creativity, and spontaneity, for in the finding of this fellowship he has also found his deepest self. The individual is given all the freedom that he needs by a community completely concerned with his fullest development and truest good while he in turn uses his freedom with all the responsible concern of Christian *agape*.

On the other hand, every individual in his responsible concern for the common good appreciates the order that is conducive to the highest co-operative living. The fellowship and the individual can therefore work out a system where the means and media of communal life abet to a maximum degree the co-operative spirit. The will to live has become a will to love; the will to power, a will to fellowship; the will to superiority, a will to service; the will to social recognition, a will to social responsibility and concern.

Two questions ought to be asked of this solution. The first is this: Have we not solved the conflict between the self and society simply by eliminating the self? Are we not talking about a selflessness which is, in effect, a will to die? The answer to this question is that the self does lose himself in the sense that his primary object of attention and end of interest become the welfare of others. But to whatever extent he does lose himself, not only is society that much better off, but he himself finds a new lease on life, a new peace and power, a new and deeper satisfaction. Paradoxically, therefore, just as happiness cannot be gained by direct seeking for it, so the deepest self can never be found except as we lose it. There is no satisfying selfish desire; the more it is supposedly satisfied the more demanding and impoverished it becomes. Yet the one who lives outside himself for the common welfare, not as a selfish seeker but as a concerned individual, becomes ever deeper, richer, and more content. Naturally he is still a real individual, for though the self is no longer its own primary end it becomes for this very reason the most responsible self, particularly with regard to the kind of responsibility it has for its own person. Such an individual offers in concern for society the best possible individual self that he can contribute, and experiences in himself the deepest possible satisfactions to enrich and ennoble the common fellowship. The more valuable and unique each individual in a community, the richer is that community; and no creative community can ever do without individual initiative, responsibility, and fulfillment. But just the same, the conflict between the will to self in the sense of a frustrating individualism has now given way to the organic fulfilling of the self in the fellowship, to a fulfilling, indeed, which is higher than the merely organic; for it is on the *super-organic* level of insight, persuasion, and personal purpose.

The second question can be briefly answered. It is this: Even if we have solved the problem theoretically, is not that a far cry from a practical or actual solution? That is true. The primary

Christian claim, however, is not theoretical but practical. It is that there *is* a power not our own that can lift and lead us into the reality of this fellowship. As a matter of fact, the full claim is that this basic conflict cannot be solved apart from the grace of God which becomes operative as a saving force only when men seek first the Kingdom of God. Even man's failure can thus be indicative of the rightness of the Christian claim. And there are those who have showed us the power of Christian love when men surrender themselves fully to it. And many there are who know how much better their lives could be if they availed themselves more often and more fully of this power. Christianity definitely does not offer to solve this problem theoretically alone, and stresses, therefore, that little has been done until the hearts of men as well as all their social patterns are increasingly subject to the claim of God's *agape*. This is the route to the better life and the new world. This is the *locus of solution* of man's problems. To depart from it is to fail; to walk in it is to find real victory.

What is lost, therefore, is not the self but the aristocratic, self-sufficient individual; and not the relevance of Christianity to our actual conflicts but the claim that the actual conflicts have no solution in terms of either theory or transforming power.

The facts suggest that God made man with this will to self, with this will to independence, and gave him with it his proper measure of freedom in order that man might be a real individual. God then conditioned both man's will and circumstance by an intrinsic need for fellowship. Only freedom in fellowship would do. This freedom in fellowship, moreover, would be shallow apart from a common need to share suffering and sacrifice, and, above all, apart from the divine and the eternal dimension. Only God as *agape* could be the adequate basis of that fellowship which alone can fully satisfy man's deepest needs.

This thought is too important not to be stressed. Perhaps we might state it in the following way: Without real persons there can be no fellowship, and persons are not made but grow. God, therefore, seems to have made man free in order that he might be responsible, and to have given him a drive for independence in order that he might be a real person, but to have let this drive be so vitally conditioned by man's need for community that the struggle within self and society and between self and society must go on until the need for God's *agape* as the basis and the dynamics of the only fully saving kind of community be both understood and accepted. The inexhaustible words of Jesus are still true. Only he that loses his life shall find it.

Contrasting with the Christian idea of outgoing concern, *agape,* is the Greek idea of the self's seeking values for the sake of realizing his best self. This idea is called *eros.* Some have thought that these two ideas stand in direct contrast and possess no functional unity.[1] If our above suggestion is right, however, God's *agape created eros* in order to make persons real, but made their basic thirst one for fellowship in God on the basis of His own nature. This, then, is their functional unity: *Eros* must precede *agape* as the dominant drive in man in order that a fellowship of real persons might be created. (This is a clue to the understanding of the problem of evil, of what is called "the fall.") But even after *agape* becomes man's primary will, *eros* has a necessary function within it. When *eros* finds its seeming death in *agape*, it is not destroyed but rather transformed. It is lost as self-centered need and found as man's felt need to be remade in terms of *agape.* The direction of *eros* toward man is kept but its content is radically changed. *Eros* still pulls toward man, but it pulls a new kind of load. In *eros* man merely uses God as the symbol of his security,

[1] Cf. Nygren, *Agape and Eros.*

as the means for his success, as the light to still his fear of the unknown. In *agape*, however, man wants to be used by God, his heart overflows with gratitude and joy for what God is for the whole world, and he longs to serve his fellow men better and to become a better member of the Christian fellowship. *Eros* is thus neither merely destroyed nor simply developed but is qualitatively transformed, not in the direction but in the content of its need.[2] *Agape* has thus both created *eros* for a definite purpose and also continues to use it by virtue of its radical transformation.

The second problem of the individual is that social order tends to suppress freedom, thwart spontaneity, and stifle initiative. The need for unity often carries with it a dread of variety. Government based on fear and force, for instance, does not take kindly to spontaneity in creative directions. Drastic regimentation in all spheres of life is supposed to be the inevitable corollary of a planned society. On the other hand, undue individualism is harmful to the general good, is usually unconcerned about the victims of the social order, and tends toward a tolerance based on indifference and toward a liberalism built on the desire to "let well enough alone." This problem runs from the one extreme of complete regimentation to the other of heedless anarchy. Between these two, various forms of solution have been tried.

About this second problem, too, Christianity has something definite to say, for it insists that, whether we consider groups of individuals or large cultural units, the more the whole community is objectively, realistically concerned with each individual and group, and each individual and group with the whole

---

[2] Richard Niebuhr has shown that a similar relation obtains between revelation and natural religion.

community, the more unity is possible—a unity not only consistent with, but creative of, the maximum variety. Christianity as *agape* is a pure form of experience that yet has a real bond of unity. Within it can be realized an almost unlimited historic variety, cultural, artistic, educational, literary, religious, social, political, economic; the only limit being that it harbor no ill will, no removable ignorance, and no indifference. As a pure form of experience its specific historic content is not predetermined in any way. Christianity combines authority and motivation with cultural pluralism, and this problem confronts modern man with peculiar urgency.

If "realized" is defined, therefore, to mean "created according to general principles and possibilities" and "actualized" is taken to mean "copied in history from some heavenly pattern," Christianity means realization rather than actualization. There is in Christianity, on the other hand, a definite unity, since God Himself is the changeless authority and since all men through Him are made to be brothers responsibly and redemptively concerned with one another. In God we are made to be one body after the pattern of Christ, and this steady pattern is yet a dynamic attitude of united concern by all and each for each and all, an organic union within one body which has many members with varying gifts and functions.

This solution is thoroughly practical for the problem can never be solved merely in terms of education. This basic human problem requires for its solution a continual approximation to *agape* in spirit as well as in theory inasmuch as the social situation is made up of attitudes, dispositions, and wills as well as knowledge and social patterns. Good social patterns require the right kind of people if they are to function desirably. While social patterns should be conducive to social co-operation, only the co-operative and concerned spirit, in the long run, produces patterns consistent with it. Thus throughout, *agape* is needed to solve the problems, for although knowledge does not guarantee good purpose, *agape*, just because it is concrete other-concern, demands all possible knowledge of the objective situation and the very best means for its desirable transformation. Christian *agape* provides, therefore, a principle of unity, both cosmic and social, that is not only consistent with enriching variety but concretely creative of it. The Christian fellowship is full and free only as all its members and groups realize within its dependable bond of unity their fullest creative spontaneity.

Christianity, then, without being in any way individualistic, but fully organic even on the super-level of personal purpose and free fellowship, includes and fulfills all the strong points of individualism. A Christian individual must be his own true self. No one else can take his place. If he suffers, the fellowship suffers in and with him. If he is irresponsible or hard of heart, that cell of the body is sick. If he is negligent or self-concerned, the community is there drained of power rather than helped with his strength. There is no individual at an instant completely unrelated to the common ways of humanity. Each one either adds health, peace, power, courage, and creative novelty or else he holds the community back or lives actually on it as a parasite. Each individual either invests with profit to the fellowship his social and spiritual inheritance, or else he squanders it. Each individual can give to society at least one good Christian, and by all the laws of reality he gives much more than that. By being radically a Christian he becomes a savior of society. What could not God do through one individual if he were completely open to God and wholly living for Him and thus for the world! We may not become the sun of the world in the daylight of which all rejoice, but we can all be light-bulbs and make a great difference to the dark corners of the world.

Christianity needs the best possible individuals, but knows that they cannot be their best except as they become through God organically one with the world.

As far as unity and variety are concerned, Christianity then says not only "be loyal to God and to the welfare of all men," but also "be thy true self that society may be true and creative through you and thus enrich the whole community." Although we are not here especially concerned with groups, whether racial, religious, national, or cultural, the same principle holds good for them as well as for individuals.

The individual, however, can enrich the common good particularly in three ways. First of all, he can pray. True and deep prayer is today almost a lost art. Christian prayer is fellowship with God, whether in meditation, thanksgiving, or petition, where we behold the greatness of God and become partakers of that greatness, where we see the patience of God and become partakers of that patience, where we understand the purpose of God and make ourselves servants of that purpose, where we discover the creative joy and power of God and become endowed with His creative joy and power, where we feel the love of God for the world and begin to taste something of that concern which lifts us out of our smallness and narrowness, out of our self-concern and indifference, into a broadening and deepening compassion for men as individuals and as society.

Then, too, the individual can contribute to the common good both by study and by work. It is very easy to underestimate the evils of the world which spring from ignorance. Dullness is a root of much social trouble as well as of individual failure. Most people read enough and too much. Light reading is a modern disease enfeebling civilization. By fast reading and little meditation most people become superficial and vague. Real study means the patient, thorough exploration of problems of life and thought until real understanding and depth is obtained. We need to learn by heart in the deepest sense of that word, and not merely by rote. Today there are open to us information and interpretation beyond any previous time in history, yet the men and women are few and far between who speak with authority on any subject by their sheer insight and control of the deeper aspects of the problem. The world today needs real students; and if we are truly Christians our indifference or preference for the entertaining, the ephemeral, and the immediately useful must give way to the patient investigation and deepening of ourselves that will dispel the limited vision, the partial loyalties, the false commitments, and drive away by the sun of truth the mists of misunderstanding that all too generally make good intention and sacrificial living demonic rather than divine.

The same is true of work. How much initiative the family, the local community, the national life, and the international scene call for. There is more goodness in people than we dream of, if it were only guided right, and used creatively. But few want to "stick their necks out," to use the vulgar but vivid phrase, and few want to co-operate with those who have the temerity to do so. Yet history owes much of its progress in every realm to individuals who dare to try and keep trying. Our present history has much light available though not effectively appropriated either generally in total attitudes and commitments or by great individuals who can appeal to the bravest and best in people and rally them for a day.

The failure of "Christianity" is to no little extent the failure to produce great leaders who themselves follow great lights. History follows to a large extent the paths chosen for it by great men. But only those are truly great who see what paths to follow. Christianity to be real must produce great leaders who combine the utmost loyalty to the common good with the maximum creative variety and adventurous novelty. Christianity possesses a vital principle of novelty. Even with a unity based on the absolute authority of God, Christianity can say, precisely because of what God is and wants: Be thy true self; be creative and enrich society; find thy freedom by means of such prayer, study, and work that combine initiative and spontaneity with responsible concern for the common good.

We have tried to suggest how Christianity offers solutions to the conflicts between the individual and society both in terms of the struggle between the will to self and the need for fellowship and in terms of the tension between the need for creative variety and social order. When all is said and done, however, the fact remains that there is no solution on the merely human level. That is why mere vision is not enough, nor is even the moralistic stress on loyalty.

Agape may seem to some to solve the problems even if it were lowered to the human level, and many accept *agape* as the highest ethical ideal without, however, feeling the need for, or understanding the necessity of, its divine dimension. The most high is to them not necessarily the most real. But the individual is a creature who knows the future, who is haunted by the transiency of all things earthly, who must find, for the meaning and destiny of anything that compels him with absolute validity, an anchorage in the absolute reality. The problems of time are solved only in eternity. That is why all enlightened humanisms fail in the end. Man is made for God, and, deep down in his heart, he cannot escape that fact. Only faith in the absolute, only religious motivation, is adequate. The merely relative becomes optional and powerless.

It is quite all right to talk about the value of man, co-operation, the unity of mankind, and to belabor totalitarianism, in-which the more it is accepted the less fanatical men do actually become. Moralism at white heat can be most dangerous. Prophetism apart from *agape* can be blindly one-sided and destructive. Every cause except Christianity seems either limited or compromising, for if it is pressed to the absolute point as *concrete, unlimited action*, it becomes fanatical. It does not by its very nature organically include every other cause.

Take truth as an absolute. Theoretically one can be completely committed to truth and allow everyone else to hold his truth. But no *content* of truth except *agape* can be acted upon with absolute commitment without becoming fanatical. The one who finds moralism as the content of absolute truth must either act upon it absolutely and thus become fanatical or else curb his absolute in social practice. The same thing happens, for instance, to the Mohammedan who should by the content of his truth compel others to become Mohammedans. As a matter of fact, when people say that they make truth their absolute, they actually mean that they make tolerance its content, in the sense that each one can theoretically believe what he finds to be true, but not act upon it if it be socially destructive. Absolute *agape* is absolute concern and co-operation. There can never be too much of this either in thought or in deed. Thus truth as the absolute amounts to the agreement either that the absolute should not be acted upon *absolutely*, no matter what man finds it to be, or else that since no one absolute is generally agreed upon each one ought to be allowed to believe as he pleases, provided he be socially co-operative in action. *Agape,* however, can be held with complete positiveness both theoretically and practically. *Agape* unites organically faith and life.

Christian *agape* is never fanatical, never merely tolerant, and never in the slightest sense negative. Since Christian *agape,* if fully realized, is complete self-giving concern for each and all by each and all, the more absolute it becomes as a reality in fellowship the better it is for that fellowship. But even in relation to an ignorant and evil world *agape* can be stressed absolutely, for since it is concern for all others where they are, it always takes people where they are and leads them in the best way to the truth whether in faith or in life. The more *agape* one has the more objective is the analysis of the situation, for to do the best for the people it must know their situation as fully as possible. The more fully *agape* is thereafter applied, the more the best method is found and used to change the undesirable situation.

Agape can trust people with freedom because it knows that God is that and has made them for that. It can trust them to investigate the truth for they know that God is that and that the way of salvation is that. It can boldly oppose with wisdom and patience all evil because it knows that God is on their side and that men are deep down made for the good and desire it. It can use constructive force without resort to mass violence or fanatical trust in physical force for it knows that God has so made men, their experience, and the laws of nature and history that all things in the end conspire toward fellowship on the basis of *agape*. It never leaves things alone through indifference or to escape bother. *Agape* never tires of caring and of showing compassion, of correcting and reforming, of bringing in a new will and a new light wherever it is and as far as it reaches. *Agape* always strives for the truth, but is always humble, never quarreling, never offensive, never sensitive, never domineering, never defensive.

In short, the more you live *agape* the more teachable you are and the better you can teach, the more you can be helped and the more you can help the world about you. Here is an

3. Christianity and the Church

A TRULY RADICAL CHRISTIANITY THAT IS DETERMINED TO make unstinted application of its root meaning ought to subject itself to a genuinely searching self-examination. It must thoroughly understand and appraise its relation to God, its relation to the institution which it has created, and its relation to the world as a whole. At the outset it may be well to lay down certain basic principles before proceeding to their elaboration and examination. In God's will the Church has its source and standard; in Jesus' life and teaching of *agape* it has its criterion for what is proper to its own peculiar fellowship; and in its organic relation to the world as a whole it knows that it can never be its own end, even under God, without being also a means for the transformation of the world.

In relation to God's will the Church is a divine and eternal fellowship. God's will, moreover, is for fellowship on the basis of *agape* and is done in history whenever and to whatever measure his will for this kind of fellowship is concretely done on earth as it is in heaven. The Kingdom of God, therefore, is actually present in history to whatever extent God's will for fellowship is concretely accepted.

Is there, however, any Christian Church in history in the sense of a fellowship actually dominated through and through by *agape*? Is it not true that no such actual fellowship exists and that very likely it never has existed in the history of the world? Was not even the first "Christian" fellowship, according to the New Testament, full of sub-Christian attitudes and ambitions? What if we had actually known those people in all their weaknesses and sins! Do we not see even within our own lives and in the lives of most church members, whatever be their profession as to conversion and a new creaturehood in Christ, that "Christians" generally are not qualitatively differ- ent from the world? However much they may differ in customs and conventions, do they differ radically in the depths of their attitudes toward themselves and their world? Have we not found to our great grief that even some religious leaders who are popularly known for their saintliness, when known in- timately, are personally ambitious, conceited and headstrong, selfishly sensitive, and anything but constantly overflowing with the self-forgetfulness of *agape*? Few and far between, we have to confess, are the saints who are so buried with God in Christ that their whole lives are constantly transfigured by His resurrection power. We do not take for granted that church members as a matter of course put the general good before their own. And if there are saints inside the church, do we not also know some of the most self-effacing, understanding, and generous people outside it?

Unless we have a genuine answer to the question whether or not the Christian Church as a fellowship in history on the basis of *agape* is merely an abstraction, our whole discussion is without real relevance to the pressing problems of our day. Let us at once admit, therefore, that there is in history no com- munity concretely and overwhelmingly dominated by *agape*. Jesus was so dominated, but only a very few have dared to follow him closely. Considering the power of his life, it seems obvious that if Christians were radical they would turn the whole world right side up. There certainly is, in any case, no institution that is radically Christian. Actual Christianity has constantly succumbed to the social patterns of ordinary life rather than cleared out the debris of this decaying world by the dynamite of Christian concern.

There are, nevertheless, believing souls whose basic intention is to live in and for this fellowship. Many of these have sacrificed the beautiful flower of their loyalty on the showy altar of traditional Christianity or have had their vitality sapped by the false chanting of its servile priests. Yet in the depth of their spirit they have helped to keep alive the reality of the fellowship of intention, forgiveness, and some attainment. Multitudes have walked the broad way, but the narrow way has never been without its lonely pilgrims. These, too, have known how far away they are from the full reality of the fellowship of Christian concern, but they have also known that the faithfulness of God is greater than their faithlessness and have prayed to walk ever better in the way of Christ.

With them, moreover, is a great number of groping souls who would like to have this kind of fellowship, who acknowledge its claim on them, who worship in some sincerity and truth the God who is *agape*, who follow Christ afar off, whose lives are vaccinated to Christianity and seem incapable of catching its burning fever, who long too much for this world's goods and good wishes or are just too busy with their daily living to find that pearl of great price, Christian fellowship, for which all else is sold in great joy.

The Christian Church, however, is present to whatever extent the fellowship of faith in God and concern for man is at all actual. The Church is the Kingdom of God on earth. It may yet be as small as a mustard seed or as a bit of leaven, but it is verily present in human hearts both in forgiveness and in reception, both in much hoping and in some having. To whatever extent the meat and matter of Christ are cherished there is also the Christian Church. The Church is neither merely a matter of morality nor a matter of forgiveness, but is always a fellowship of grace and power, repudiating the standards of the world and bringing forth the better fruits of the spirit.

This relation of the Church to God can be viewed in at least four significant ways. The Church is, in the first place, the extension through history of the spirit of Jesus. It is the continuity of his kind of consciousness, the perpetuation of his purpose. Jesus showed what God is and what man ought to be if he lived in the kind of fellowship for which God made him. He gave man, to use Biblical phrases, a better hope through which to draw nigh unto God who is able to save unto the uttermost them that draw nigh unto Him. He became the the mediator of a better covenant that is founded on better promises because in Jesus God was seen to be *agape*. He made a living way to God through his teaching, living, and utter self-sacrifice. The Church is Christian in so far as it continues in history through its living witness the spirit of Jesus.

The Church is, in the second place, the extension of the Atonement. This assertion is implicit in the first but ought to be made explicit. Jesus solved, as we have seen, the conflict between the will to self and the will to fellowship in that his will to live became a will to love. His will became a will to carry the burdens of men and if need be to sacrifice his own life that men might find the positive way of fulfillment in the Christian fellowship. His holiness was not, first of all, for his own self-improvement, and much less for the negative sake of keeping himself clean from the vices of men. His holiness was, rather, a separation from the world in prayer to God that he might have a single eye and the will to walk humbly with common men in their common ways, to teach them the eternal truths, and to help them carry their daily loads. "For their sake" he sanctified himself. This is one of the greatest verses in the New Testament. It is the key to Christian conduct.

Jesus' whole life was spent to make men at one with God, to reconcile them with the One who cared the most deeply for them. The atonement that he made was based on his frank recognition that we are all created by God, belong to one body of humanity, and can never be free, healthy, or whole before the entire body is well. Here is a cell of humanity that atones creatively for the rest through free understanding of the need for it; an atonement that therefore far surpasses in beauty and power the organic functioning of the animal body. The fact that Jesus gave himself in order that men might become "at one with God" is the key to the life of the whole Christian fellowship.

Something of utmost importance happened in history when Jesus made man see and feel the power of God's love. To be a Christian, thereafter, ought to mean far more than to believe in Jesus creedally or to walk in his way morally. It must mean a willingness to suffer and to share, to give not only of what we have but our own selves even as God gave himself. Love becomes stern, realistic, objective. To be a Christian means to have a super-organic fellowship with God through Christ in terms of a common concern for the world, a concern which is of God's very essence, which was the center of Jesus' thought and life, and which constitutes the binding fabric of the Christian fellowship. The Church is the Church only as it extends the Atonement by actualizing it in history. The Church which does not suffer does not care for the world. The Church that does not give itself for the world is by that very fact not Christian. By that standard the Church must be concretely judged.

The Church is, thirdly, the embodiment in history of the

Holy Spirit. To think clearly we need to distinguish between the spirit of God and the Holy Spirit. The spirit of God is God operating on the level of creation. The Holy Spirit is God operating through a fellowship where He is understood to be *agape*. Men never fully understood that God was *agape* until Jesus came, and perhaps not before Pentecost. It may be that as the disciples then kept praying and pondering they began to understand more clearly who Jesus was, why he was the Messiah, why he knew himself to be the son of God in a conclusive way so that men could find the truth and the way only as they understood and accepted his message. God naturally *is* always the same. His spirit is always *agape*. But He *operates* differently in history according to the way that He is understood and accepted. Since before Jesus came men did not know that God in His very essence was *agape*, something new actually came into history at that point and at the point where a new kind of fellowship was born based on a new insight and saving power.

Since, therefore, the Holy Spirit operates only in a fellowship based on *agape*, the Christian Church alone is his embodiment in history. This should be the most sobering of all thoughts, yet also the most joyous, a mystery too great for mortal man, that only in the fellowship of Christian concern is God present as He really is. Naturally this truth is not exclusive but conclusive. It is not exclusive but consummate. All other experiences may be deep and beautiful—how far we can find God in nature, how far He is known in the moral law, how far He is understood through His endlessness and majesty, how far He is revealed in His patient creativity; but only in the experience of redemptive concern for mankind where we really give ourselves up that the body may be whole do we find God as He is in His inmost nature and purpose. What would happen to the Church if it constantly remembered what it is and whose it is and had as its greatest continual desire to live up to this truth in actual history?

The Church is, in the fourth place, the end for which God made the world. It has been popular to think of the Church as a mere means to the coming of the Kingdom of God. Yet in so far as the Church is the Church it is the Kingdom present on earth. How severely those are now criticized who used to think of the Kingdom of God in terms of a new social order built along Christian principles. Perhaps they were too optimistic, perhaps they did forget the deeper dimensions of the Kingdom; yet withal they were right in their contention that the Kingdom by its very nature must radically challenge all evil social relations and express, though not exhaust, itself in their transformation. Even at its holiest and best the Church is a means to the bringing in here and now of better social attitudes and structures. Social relations are the nature of ultimate stuff. They are the core of reality. Social relations on the basis of Christian concern constitute the purpose of God for the world. They are God's end in creation. All else is secondary to this kind of fellowship in the light of which all else must be interpreted for its significance. In an organism each end is also a means. In a fellowship all are intrinsically related and live for one another. Even God, in fact, is both an end and a means. He is the only self-existent end and yet the chief means in man's salvation.

God's *agape* takes the way of the cross for our sake that His suffering might effect the final organic fellowship in which all are united first by a common experience of need and of suffering, and then at last by a common victory and a common joy. The crown, the fellowship, is the end of creation; the cross is the means to effect that end. The Church of Christ knows the joy of victory even now. It knows that God has triumphed over sin and death. The Church must proclaim Christ as victor. Even now we know God's final victory and our whole lives must overflow with this victory. The Church without thanksgiving and joy is no Christian Church. The Church experiences at the same time both suffering for the world and joy over God's salvation as a mother bending over her desperately sick child both weeps and rejoices when she hears that it is going to recover. This must be the clearest note of the Church. Without it, it will fail to convince a sin-sick and weary world.

The Church as the actualization of God's purpose in history is thus also both an end and a means, right now experiencing both common sufferings and the joy set before it. It is the "anticipated attainment" of the purpose of God even while it strives to attain that purpose. By being the means to a new kind of community the Church also realizes the end of creation of which it is even now itself an earnest.

Our second main point in this chapter deals with the relation of the Church to the institution which it has created. Under this topic we ought to point out, first of all, that the Church as an institution is itself under the judgment of the Christian criterion, *agape*. Some are now saying that the Church in writing the New Testament created the Christ figure, that the Church is God's primary revelation in history and that all doctrines are merely the expression of the Church's life and can, therefore, be judged by it. We believe this interpretation to be wrong both historically and systematically. The most natural historic interpretation of the inbreaking of the understanding of *agape* as central in cosmos and conduct is that it came through one great figure who thus in fact founded the fellowship on the basis of *agape*. The more one ponders this question the more one realizes how willing some people are to sacrifice Jesus to a method of historical investigation or to a philosophic theory. But Jesus, himself, cannot be done away with as the primary figure.

Systematically, moreover, whichever way God did become known as *agape*, this is the standard of Christian faith and fellowship, which, though never fully attained, yet always remains the criterion of Christian truth and conduct. The primary revelation is God as *agape* and this alone judges the institutional Church. This explains in part why the Bible is almost worshiped by great groups of Christians. They have sensed the truth that the Word has not only been made flesh but has also been objectified in history as the record of a permanent criterion. The word preached and lived by the Church must always be judged by the objectification in the Bible of the Word made flesh, but this Word is none other than God's *agape* revealed to man in Christ. Though the Church is the main form and living continuity of the revelation, it is not the highest authority of God's revelation. If *agape* is merely a contingent theoretical development of the Church's life and not rather the determinative standard of its faith and conduct, the absoluteness of the Christian claim that God is *agape* is reduced to the secondary significance of a relative group rationalization and to the sociological mysticism of conventional creativity. The Church is, to be sure, not primarily a theory but a living community; but this living community is itself subject to a changeless standard by the embodiment of which alone it can continue to be Christian.

In the second place, the Church and the institution must not be equated outright. The Church is an intensive fellowship of those who sincerely accept God as *agape* in faith and life.

Faith in God as *agape* is the only generator of the Christian fellowship and its only standard. The institution, on the other hand, is an extensive fellowship. The Church is an organism. The institution is an organization. We must be clear on this point for there is a definite distinction between the external institution and the Church consisting of those who, though failing before God, yet daily surrender themselves to Him in a fellowship of forgiveness, in deep humility and penitence, and seek for that "city which hath foundations whose builder and maker is God."

This distinction is important, for the only standard of membership in the Christian Church is fellowship on the basis of faith in God as *agape*. This refers to modes of baptism, church orders, communion, and all the rest. They are definitely and decidedly secondary questions in comparison to the one eternal Christian criterion. There are undoubtedly real Christians even outside the institutional churches. There are perhaps legions who cannot accept the primitive myths of the actual churches, who are nauseated by their social sterility, their compromising cowardice, and their downright selfish fear and divisiveness, perhaps even many Mohammedans, Hindus, Confucians, and Jews, who have become persuaded that God wants to create a fellowship of responsible concern, and who try to live it day by day, even though some of these cannot own the name because they see little actual relation between the reality of the fellowship in God and that which is preached and practiced by the institutional churches.

Many of us, perhaps, have known saints who do not belong to the institutional church because they feel that organized Christianity generally misrepresents the fellowship which Jesus taught, lived, and died for. Are not these organically one with us, though they cannot share even our faltering faith in the institution? Are we not rather under their judgment? Surely they are joined with us through God in eternal reality and separated only through historic misunderstanding. They are far closer to us than those who belong to the institution and may even support it heavily through a misunderstanding of its ideal nature, and who would indeed be appalled if *agape* were taken seriously as the necessary standard of all human relations. From these we are in truth separated in the essentials and joined only in the outward allegiance to the institution. The real standard of membership in the Christian Church, in any case, is not the institution but the genuine fellowship of *agape* through faith in God.

Does this then mean that the institution is unimportant and that allegiance to it can be taken lightly? It does mean, we repeat, that the supreme allegiance is to the reality of the fellowship and not to the half-sprawling, half-straddling institution which is greatly the product of demonic forces and reactionary interests, not only of a social, political, and economic character but also, far worse, of a religious and spiritual nature, that even in great parts denies the ultimacy of God's *agape* as the only standard and reason for the existence of the Christian fellowship. It does mean, too, that no institution has authority over the interpretation of the Christian faith and can reduce its radicalness by one iota. One individual who understands the once-for-all given Christian revelation has the right to shake by that insight the whole institution. That revelation is not static but dynamic, not closed but permanently open. This truth is a clear and insistent challenge to prophets of our day to wake the institution and cleanse it by the fiery judgment of the Christian truth. When all this is said, however, it must always be kept in mind that a basic answer to a basic human need becomes expressed and perpetuated through some form of organization. The vital spirit becomes embodied in history. The Church creates an institution, and we cannot avoid that problem.

As there is no discarnate spirit in human history, so there is no discarnate church. Our real question is, therefore, whether we shall support this institution as it is, change it, or create a new one. When we are tempted to accept the last choice, we remember, however, how the reformers and founders of new institutions usually end up by having founded another sect. But we definitely cannot accept the situation as it is. The institution must be reformed or destroyed. The storms of our era may continue to sweep away an apostate organization. We hope, however, that there is yet time to change it. The only rule for doing this is that the relation between the Church and the institution must be as organic as possible. The present organization or lack of adequate organization reveals a heavily wounded spirit. The Church is desperately sick and cannot heal its own body. One of the severest diseases is professional denominationalism. Loyalty to a sect when it retards in any way the coming of the one true Church of Jesus Christ is idolatrous. Every refusal to co-operate organically as far and quickly as possible, from the largest sect, the Roman, to the smallest group in an isolated hamlet, is a direct refusal of Christian fellowship. The social patterns of sectarianism are directly conducive to division. What is the use of praying "lead us not into temptation" while steadily refusing to remove the objects of temptation? Federalism may have to precede organic union. That seems necessary in view of concrete obstacles due to divergent historical inheritance. But time is short and we must go as fast as we possibly can toward the goal. Denominations can still be orders within the church maintaining the beauty of historic variety and creativity. Unity is far different from uniformity. Ecclesiastical totalitarianism is hardly less attractive than its political counterpart. But the Christian Church is one organism and must express that fact in its organization.

The deepest failure, of course, is not the failure of organization but the failure of the Christian Church to be a vital Christian fellowship. Organization is important for in an ideal organization the patterns of reaction are conducive to co-operation. Common interests and responsibilities tend to draw people together. But organization is not enough. It is not even primary. What shall it profit us to organize narrowness and divisiveness and lose our soul? We must have indispensably a new, sweeping Christian revival which is bigger than the old conversionism and deeper than the old social gospelism. The full vision and all-around responsibility of the Christian faith must be preached in life and power until it calls man to penitence before God and to an all-transforming social responsibility. We may have to start with prophetic individuals who can lead because they know how to follow the only true light. We may have to have live cells of Christian community springing up like oases within our parched churches. These intensive groups of Christian fellowship will prescribe for themselves ways of walking together that spring out of a burning concern for people in all their troubles and sorrows. Groups of concrete fellowship centered around study, prayer, and work may give the vision and power that can effect a Christian institution. There must also come a new prophetic preaching deeply rooted in the Christian Gospel that will show the Church and the world what Christianity really is. Yet we return to assert that no preaching or preacher's project can ever take the place of groups filled with the spirit which realistically and perseveringly set out to show the way of the Christian fellowship.

The final relation of the Church is to the world. Unavoidably in treating this topic we must picture an ideal Church with an ideal institution in its relation to this actual world, and keep in mind that this then represents only *the locus of solution.*

First of all, the Church should unconditionally condemn all evil while genuinely acknowledging that it stands itself under the same judgment and that it needs itself the constant forgiveness of God. The message of the Church should never be a compromise message. There is no place for political expediency and for cautious accommodation in the truth that the Church proclaims. The Church must always speak the full truth of Christ in love. The word "Christian" must be kept unreservedly and unexceptionally for the ideal which God is and demands, by which we are judged, and to which we must be saved. There is no place for a church that has lost the tang of its saltiness. Such a church is a conspiracy against the community, a parasite sucking its blood while offering nothing essential to its life.

The word "Christian," and we said to begin with, must keep its highest meaning. War is never Christian. A lawsuit is never Christian. These reveal our failure to be Christian. If all were Christian, these things would obviously never exist or occur. To call war, divorce, or any other act exhibiting basic failure of fellowship Christian, even under the circumstances, is to lose sight of the reality of the Christian fellowship as a redemptive dimension of basic discontinuity with the general level of human failure. True Christianity is a radically new creaturehood and radically transformed social attitudes and relations. What we may do because of the hardness of our hearts may be necessary, the world being what it is, but let us never reduce the word Christian, or the message of the Church, to this level. We are a city set on a hill. It is no use to plead the excuse that we *cannot* live up to the Christian ideal. The Christian ideal stands as an actual demand, and when we fail to incarnate it in spirit and deed we must not only ask for forgiveness but also for new strength to come ever closer to this ideal. If pedagogy requires the milk rather than the meat of the Gospel, let only the meat be termed Christian. Self-righteousness and complacency have been increased by our calling "the easy wrong" rather than "the hard right" Christian. We do ourselves and society no service by reducing the full challenge of Christian truth. If we sought God's Kingdom first, moreover, and lived more deeply in the Holy Spirit, we should also have a concrete Christian fellowship that would utterly surprise our faithless hearts.

Having preached the full Gospel and not hidden its truth in a napkin, the Church should, in the second place, offer forgiveness, pardon, and healing to confused and weary men. This the Church can do if it preach not itself, but God's salvation that reaches genuinely into the depths of man's everyday problems as well as into his basic spiritual conflicts. The prophetic ministry must be overarched by the ministry of healing which has all the resources of eternity at hand. The Church is not first of all a means to immediate social progress, but is above all a well of healing for man's crises in the divine dimension. The church that loses its faith in the eternal is no longer a church but a club. The message of the church that condemns unsparingly is by its very nature the message that utterly saves. The searching light of the absolute comes to give absolution to the sin-sick souls of men.

In the third place, the Church should indoctrinate its members, especially the young, not only with the faith that in saving gives steadiness and creativity to human lives, but also with the ideals of a Christian society and a Christian world. It is the duty of the Church to give light and direction. There are Christian ideals for society, and these must be taught as such. Whenever, therefore, churchmen become pedagogical and try concretely to span the chasm between the full Christian ideals and social or political action—that is, try to work out "middle axioms" for practical "Christian" programs—they are under divine obligation to explain to their people that these objectives are not fully Christian. Adequate motivation comes not from the absoluteness of the political proposals but from the absolute demand upon each Christian that he do the will of God. If the sub-Christian nature of political action is made definitely clear, there is likely to be little bitterness and disillusionment later on. The Christian ideal, the historic actual, and the concretely possible ought all to be taught for what they are.

This means, in the fourth place, that the Church as the Church ought never to back any specific social or political program as Christian, but only as a move toward it. Perhaps the Church ought not even to do this as a church, but rather to provide the moral energy, the vital motivation, and the needed drive to effect social improvement. The Church should, in any case, raise up prophets in all areas of activity, wise, patient leaders who will deal with the actual and the relevantly possible in the full light of the Christian ideal. The Church should also give stimulus to groups within itself to work out desirable social patterns. These groups should work within the Church, at the same time acknowledging the source of its endeavor and the fact that it is not working as the Church. Within the Church there can be accomplished wholesome political work if the Church remains the mother that keeps the children within her home, giving them both enough freedom and initiative for creative choice and enough responsibility to bind them together in common concern for common objectives. Surely groups like the Fellowship of Reconciliation, Religion and Labor, Socialist Christians, the Cooperative Movement, or a different type of movement, more indirect, like the Oxford Group, and any political point of view, provided it be genuinely constructive, ought to be held within the Church. Christian *agape* is big enough for differing approaches to the solving of common problems and to the attaining of common goals. We have almost taken for granted the defeatist position that all concrete social struggles must be fought out outside the Church. The greatest hope for mankind, however, lies in a united Church that will produce both the direction and the drive for the organic solution of the world's problems by the very depth of its fellowship in, to, and for God. When the Church solves its own problems it can give immediate and effective help to the solving of the world's problems.

The largest gain of the Christian Church during the last hundred years, apart from its emancipation from a binding, unintelligent, and a divisive literalism, is its awakening to a general social responsibility. The Church now knows beyond recall that Christianity covers not only all men but also all relations of men. This new consciousness is itself, nevertheless, greatly in danger of becoming prostituted for immediate political ends which seem Christian in theory but which when they are embodied in history become themselves demonic and stand in need of judgment. We repeat, therefore, that the primary function of the Church is not social reform. This is enormously important, as we shall see in the next chapter. The first function of the Church, nevertheless, is making God known and effective in the hearts of men.

Some Christians actually talk as though a capitalist were by his very nature and position excluded from the Church of God while others are no less certain that labor organizers are spoiling the peace and prosperity of God's good world and ought certainly not to claim the decency of the Christian Church. The Church, however, is for all men and for all conditions of men, now and forever. Here men must find the answer to their spiritual problems. Here they must meet God and face eternity. Here they must feel the judgment of God upon their daily lives. Here they must receive His pardon, His care, and His help. Here they must find a fraternity of incentive, patience, and understanding. Whenever, therefore, one culture stratum is made predominant, and its language becomes the customary language of the pulpit including its critical attitudes toward other culture strata; whenever one set of interests and attitudes become a divisive theme so that the holders of different interests and attitudes are by their very circumstances driven away, there the Christian fellowship is broken. The Church must speak a common language and aim at common objectives answering the deepest needs that men have in common because they are all children of the heavenly Father, members of a common fellowship, and servants bound to a common Master. The Church must be big enough for all, open enough for all needs, and strong enough to give to all those symbols of security that stand for the final truth and controlling reality that cannot be shaken.

4. Christianity and Society

ONE OF THE MOST BURNING QUESTIONS OF TODAY IS THE relation of Christianity to society. The times are so urgent that the temptation of such dogmatism as often accompanies critical decisions lies close at hand. This analysis tries, however, to avoid both this danger and that of merely theoretical discourse by the taking of the absolute standard of Christian faith, God as *agape*, or Christian love, and applying it with such insight as we possess to the three critical problems of modern society. These are education, economics, and world order.

Today education is suffering a heavy barrage of criticism from practically all sides. From the side of religion the heaviest is the accusation that we have tried to educate people into the Kingdom of God whereas only genuine repentance and moral renewal will do. It is true that education has, consciously or unconsciously and to a surprising extent, identified knowledge with virtue. This has been due not only to the natural way in which each profession tends to think of its own job as most important (and how easy it is for those of us who teach to take for granted that teaching will save the world!), but also to a false philosophy of history and human nature where the depths and stubbornness of evil were not sufficiently acknowledged; to a sophisticated negativism that produced critical and clever but seldom appreciative and creative minds; and to an analytical method that worshiped quantitative measurements and sense proofs while it came close to losing man's peculiar heritage, the creative and the spiritual, and nearly allowed his creative and intangible capacities to atrophy.

It is unnecessary, moreover, to use a strict definition of education, for we can think of it as including all of man's consciously fostered reactions, whether of thought, emotions, or will. If we do, we see that with the incoming of our greater knowledge of man and of social laws education must take on greater scope and significance. Not to recognize the potential power of education for good and bad in the modern world is surely to be blind. Nor must even formal education be limited to the public schools. From the Christian point of view in its inevitable concern for society there are at least four aspects of education which are of first-class importance.

The first is education in the home. The family is both a natural and an inescapable unit of education. Here the children receive their first, and very likely deepest, impressions for life. Children learn prodigiously through imitation and suggestion. What counts the most heavily is what the parents are and do each day from morning to night. Parents can consciously teach Christianity by being Christian. Perhaps the biggest single channel for preparing the right social attitudes, and one that is immediately and constantly available to millions upon millions of people, is the making of Christian homes. This must not be a hit-or-miss affair, but one with which the Church and every family must be consciously and diligently concerned. What the world needs most is the return to cosmic authority and absolute moral standards. Without these society breaks down. But these come only as the intrinsic content of a great faith. Great faith, however, comes extremely hard apart from its being part of the child's deepest early impressions. Atheism is practically fostered where the family is not religious both in deed and in open confession. These families indoctrinate their children in unbelief in the most effective way possible. Hence the sophisticated skepticism that has brought us to "the edge of the abyss." Family training is so lastingly effective that religious education has an almost insurmountable handicap when children have been brought up to be irreligious. As far as religion goes there is no neutral territory. Either God or atheism is constantly being taught. And the deepest teaching is by life itself. The life must still be the light. Any Christian strategy for a better society must, therefore, include this basic program of a return to family worship and religious living for the sake of our children and our children's children. Character comes less by words than by deeds, but a combination of both is best.

A way can and must be found. Parents themselves must worship. Religion must become part of the everyday routine from rising to setting sun. Religious objects of art and affection must color family life and imagination. The radio and the phonograph can furnish new means of family worship and instruction. The Church must know how to capitalize on such tools for nourishing the religious life. Great hymns can be sung daily, forming bedrock moral foundations for growing children. It is surprising how much children learn indirectly in this way, and how much they retain throughout life. Those who have had this experience feel very deeply about it. They know how the great songs of the Church combine symbolic motivation with socially important ideas.

At a very early age children can use both silence and discussion. Parents can read great books and stories with ever more eager children. It is amazing how delighted children will be with the reading of the right kind of Christian biography. At the present time the writer's son, aged nine, looks forward with eager joy to the regular Sunday evening reading with his parents of Basil Mathews' *Paul, the Dauntless*. Parents can share with their children their books and interests in every sphere of life and interpret this new knowledge in Christian terms. Parents must watch wisely comic strips and radio programs and all books and entertainments lest their children fall prey to the vicious commercialism and the prostituted propaganda which constitute some of the most sinister factors of our civilization. The world in its wisdom is wise. What have we done to capture the most important approaches to our new world for wholesome living and for religious faith and commitment?

Dramatic proposals for a better world are common and popular. The careful thinker knows, however, that the home, the church, and the school are the slow but basic determiners of the world in which we live. It is, therefore, with these that we must start if we are ever basically to remake society. One of the deepest tragedies of modern history is, therefore, the failure of religious education in the churches. It did get away from a narrow traditional theology, only to land in a modernism that was rightly concerned with the child, with life, and with society, but that usually had little to teach except a thin moralism.

Progressive education as a method went to extremes which are now being generally modified by competent educators in the light of all the storms of able protest that it aroused. But the method, with all its superficial understanding of the deeper levels of historic transmission and of the primary importance of these intangible values and beliefs which make men and not animals, was nevertheless not so destructive of vital religion as was the false philosophy which generally accompanied it and which was imported in large measures by those who learned the method. As a plain matter of fact, the doors of the Christian Church were thrown wide open to a historical relativism which is not only the death of religion but, in the end, the death of vital morality and decent civilization. Never did a wolf hide more cleverly in sheep's clothing. The Church exists primarily to give men a sense of the Christian absolute and to produce the spiritual and social fruits of that sense.

Growth is good but it must be Christian growth. No experience is a Christian goal unless it be the experience of God as revealed in Jesus, the fellowship which flows from this, and the new meaning which colors all of life. Every method must be tested entirely by its capacity to make the Christian faith understood and effective. In this area the Church faces the need for one of its most crucial and drastic reformations. Religious education is essential to the Church's life. Today its task is of crucial importance. We must make much more than ever of the teaching ministry. The religious education movement itself was no mistake, as many people are now saying, but it made a very bad mistake when it went modernist. Religious education to help the Church and the world must understand and accept true or radical Christianity. Religious education must itself grow in its understanding of the Christian faith. It holds the key to a vital Christian Church, but what shall it profit unless it knows which door to open?

In the third place, the illicit marriage in general education between a narrow scientism and general truth must be broken. Its illegitimate offspring are thrown out on life ill-clad and ill-fed. All the deepest values of truth and life, our whole moral and spiritual heritage, have been gradually eaten away by the acids of sophisticated skepticism which have formed the steady diet of our pseudo-intellectuals. Deep tragedy, too, there is in the fact that these pseudo-intellectuals who have thought it smart to scoff at the very moral and spiritual foundations upon which life rests have done so not chiefly because they have had no concern for the world, nor mostly because they have occupied irresponsible positions where theory seldom met the test of social needs, nor mostly because the intellectual life without practical commitment tends to the feeling of unreality and indecision. The chief reason for their having been so sophomoric and "smart-alecky" is that deep in their lives they have been frustrated by their inability to believe anything great in the cosmic dimension. They have been overwhelmed by the spirit of the age, overly impressed by the practical prestige of science, and unable to see how costly and arbitrary are the assumptions they have made in accepting their "unconscious axioms" without adequate criticism.

Part of this is our fault. Religion has not produced profound thinkers to solve the problems of an advancing day, and the champions of a limited method were able to turn it into unlimited truth almost by default. Now, fortunately for the world, not only scientists themselves, and philosophers and theologians, but men of letters, education, and practical pursuits are in increasing numbers able to see both the problem and part of the solution. Religious thinkers, too, furnished with modern weapons from all the arsenals of truth, are on their way to a new leadership in modern civilization as men begin to understand that reason, if it is to be its fullest and most adequate self and if it is to lead society to a new steadiness and creativity, must necessarily rise from the scientific and the philosophic to the religious level. New religious life and light alone can drive out the reductionist anaesthetic of scientism and renew the moral nerve and the sense of spiritual seeing within the body of modern civilization.

Then, lastly, general education must include religious instruction. If this is not done, the churches must make every effort to provide all possible education under their auspices. Today there is, for instance, real need for colleges under religious auspices. Our religious heritage can be taught objectively—as those of us know who have been taught religion as children in public schools. Religion is that interpretation of life in which the most high is also the most real. In this Catholics, Jews, and Protestants generally agree. Protestantism, of course, is nearly powerless until it returns to that radical stream of true Christianity which will heal its divisions and put power and positive content into its faith. When this is done, the problem as to what ought to be taught is far on the road to solution.

God as *agape* must eventually become central for faith and life. All things must everywhere be seen in this steady light and in it find their deepest meaning. Public education in religion would, however, have to be confined to general areas such as God, man, and the religious sanctions and criteria for conduct. This means, of course, a frank giving up of our agnostic separation of Church and state in which our children are effectively taught that religion is not an indispensable part of life and civilization. Similar restitutions of the full curriculum ought to take place in higher education. The problems are obviously enormous on all levels of instruction, considering that a secularized and rather impotent education meets a divided and generally backward Church; but the time has come to face the full truth of our situation and then work for those revolutionary channels by which history constructively renews itself. The fact that we are far from the goal must not keep us from keeping our eye on it and heading in that direction. Whitehead stresses that the essence of all education is religious. This is the lost link in our whole social system. When it is found and rightly used, education will rise as the great moral, cultural, and religious force in the world of tomorrow.

The second major problem of modern society is its system of economics. The social patterns of our present economic system are for the most part conducive to self-interest, social irresponsibility, and hardness of heart. The social patterns of any civilization, moreover, are of enormous importance. Many individualists reduce social situations to individual attitudes and talk about individual freedom as neutral to morality. Yet the social patterns of any civilization either lead the individual into temptation or help him to overcome temptation. To say that genuine morality demands social temptations, so that it is really undermining morality to change the social patterns in favor of moral action, is as wise as saying that we should have more moral children if we did not have Christian homes where they are externally predisposed to morality.

The two best features of our present economic system are its appeal to initiative and to variety of economic goods. These features can be kept, however, within such economic patterns as encourage not conflict but co-operation. The apologetic stress on the productive capacity of the capitalistic system is hardly well taken in an age when the basic problems are those of the moral control of economics, the inalienable right of each man to work, equitable distribution, the full and humanly profitable employment of all means of production, the control of judicial and police force, the control of the agencies of propaganda, and the actual power over government. The masses are rapidly rising to power through general education, through their own organizations, and more and more, it is to be hoped, through their own news organs. They exercise increasingly great political pressure and, more or less mutely or audibly, demand economic democracy. Whatever economic patterns Christianity must work for are definitely away from those which encourage conflict and selfishness and toward those which stress concern for the common good.

A great fallacy is also abroad to the effect that economic laws must not be tampered with, lest all suffer. This is ideology, not truth. *Laissez-faire* economics uses this as a justification of the evils of our present system, calls these laws "natural," and maintains they are as a whole for the good of society. That is precisely as true as saying that laws of health are in the nature of things, and medicine tampers with the laws of life and thus weakens the race. It is precisely as true as saying that there are natural laws of human association and any and all government tampers destructively with civilization. We cannot believe that. Can we? Some actually do take these positions, of course, and *laissez-faire* philosophy is consistent in maintaining that the minimum government is the best government. But however much nostalgia we may have for primitive life, and however much we may yearn to be left alone with our enterprises, this complicated modern world cannot return except by suicide to the primitive principles of anarchy. Economic laws are controllable by man for the sake of the general good; they are understood and must be manipulated in the service of the whole society, even "unto this last." The community is responsible for each and all not only morally but also economically. The myth of the sacred independence of economic laws must be exploded to make way for the intelligent and responsible planning of economic affairs. Economic theory must become the rationalization, not of class interest, but of the general good.

The nature of property from the Christian point of view ought also to be kept in mind. For Christianity property is never static but always functional. Economic resources are the God-given means and media of fellowship. They are not first of all private possessions, but rather responsibilities entrusted to man by God for the sake of the common welfare. Property belongs, first of all, to God, has been given by Him for social purposes, and no individual or group is ever more than a steward of it. Property, moreover, is a social function, a matter not primarily of individual but of social stewardship. Primary control of property, therefore, by the very nature of things belongs under God to society as a functional whole, not to discrete individuals who then pool their resources in order to maintain order and control through the establishment of government. It is not enough to say that property is a function of the spirit that it might develop responsibility (it is that and the individual does need private property to develop responsibility); but it is even more a function of the social spirit, of the community, in order to develop social initiative, co-operation, and responsibility. Property belongs to the self as a socius, for property is primarily social in origin, function, and meaning.

The fact that social patterns precondition individual behavior and that property is a means and medium of community would seem to point emphatically to democratic socialism as the nearest approximation we can see to a Christian ideal of economic organization. Profiteering is in essence anti-Christian. What is euphemistically called "free enterprise" actually means freedom mostly for the strong—those who possess the means of production or have the skill to attain such control. There is no parallel freedom for the masses of men, but rather an oppressive preconditioning to economic, social, and cultural poverty and dependence because of this very anti-social freedom of the strong.

This economic system also produces ways of perpetuating classes and injustice of economic distribution, *regardless of ability and application*, through such devices as investment and inheritance. Some reap almost entirely what others sow. "Free enterprise," therefore, is not a little an apologetic expression to justify an unchristian system conducive to unchristian social behavior. "Private profit" tends to be an anti-social category in that the reward and use of all effort is all too often not even in general controlled in the interest of the common good. More than that, the whole motive of private profit makes for conflict instead of co-operation, for self-concern rather than for social responsibility.

The system also makes for hardness of heart, since low wages and inadequate working conditions at the worker's expense give competitive advantage, and besides develops a most self-righteous group of possessors. Even resultant charity on the part of the tender-hearted (or on the part of the diabolically astute) tends to harm both the giver and the receiver. The social patterns of private profit are painfully destructive of the very basic ideals of a Christian society and must give way to a new social system.

Socialism, that is public ownership of (or at least definite control over) all economic resources, means of production, and all other processes which directly affect the commonweal, points challengingly in a Christian direction. We must remember, too, that in the long run people tend to control as much as they own. The modern world needs democratic ownership of production for use rather than for profit, democratic control of the process of distribution, and democratic supervision over consumption. Democracy is, furthermore, primarily a matter not of geographic but of functional representation and control. New ways of government in terms of modern categories of labor, management, the professions, agriculture, distribution, and consumption need to be worked out if genuine democracy is to keep public planning and ownership (or control) from falling into the hands of evil bureaucracy or of strategic minorities who might thwart the common good.

There is, of course, a real danger that public planning and ownership (or control), instead of increasing man's cultural, intellectual, and religious freedom by making man decreasingly dependent upon the material side of life, might result in a general oppressive control of all the areas of life. We must not wink at this fact, particularly in our own heterogeneous country. But the point is this, that this does not happen in an intelligent and alert democracy which is built on moral and religious foundations. And we are here talking about a civilization endeavoring to become Christian. A society morally capable of freedom can, in any case, have it at its maximum only when the social patterns are conducive to co-operation. Socialism in modern society, granted moral energy, ought to release man for a new burst of creativity and achievement.

There are three reasons, at least, and we believe four, that our proposals can never be called radical utopianism. In the first place, history shows plainly that the world is spiraling toward socialization. As the economically less developed regions of the world shrink increasingly, unless they are kept by the force of an iniquitous imperialism from getting their own machine civilization, it will become increasingly necessary to plan and supervise our own production for use rather than for profit. In the second place, we stress that this is the goal which must be reached as quickly as possible, but that the steps must be wisely taken with proper regard to the existing conditions and attitudes. In the meantime we must work patiently but persistently for every possible improvement within our present system. In the third place, we have maintained throughout that no mere changing of systems will change the world. Social patterns affect conduct but they do not determine it. We must, therefore, have Christian individuals if we are to have a Christian society. And, fourthly, for those who believe, as we do, in the Christian faith as the final truth, the patterns we advocate are the natural implications of our faith. This last reason is of utmost importance when social motivation and standards need cosmic dynamics and foundations.

Today reactionary forces are using the specious argument that economic control by the state inevitably involves the loss of all other freedoms as well. This is not necessarily true. Rather, competitive capitalism seems doomed because of its social, moral, and international failures. Central control and planning are dangerous only if they are not thoroughly socialized, i.e., intelligently democratic, or if they try to operate without moral dynamics. The communal patterns of socialism, however, would help to abolish those attitudes which have been partly produced by this system and which if they persisted would make any system a failure. Democratic socialism has ample opportunity for popular pricing and for the development of initiative. The truth is that people do work for social reasons and would do so increasingly when conditioned to new sanctions. Naturally it would not by itself produce any saints; no system can do that. But even if reward would still in some proportion be according to ability and application, that reward would stand for a real social contribution by that individual himself within a socially planned project. This reward, furthermore, could be used for consumers' goods only, never for any investment or inheritance that could prey parasitically upon the general social good.

Socialism is certainly no panacea, but it ought to help to produce social patterns which encourage rather than discourage the Christian life. Whatever may or may not happen to Russia after this, we have all seen how prodigiously educable man is and how effective social patterns can be even within a short period of time. Christianity cannot be less socially effective than communism, and it seems altogether obvious that we Christians must from now on take more seriously the challenge to provide those economic patterns which shall be naturally conducive to a Christian society.[1]

The third major social task confronting us is the establishing of an adequate and effective world order. Many use our modern crisis to show how utterly bad man is. Without denying the fact that he cannot get along unless he first seeks the Kingdom of God, it is, however, true that much of our present chaos and destruction is due to the fact that we have no system for the intelligent and effective settling of the seething pushes and pulls of historic forces on the international scale. Dr. Vida Scudder recently pointed out, in conversation, that following the order of the Lord's Prayer, the Kingdom of God must come before men can do His will. When God's name is hallowed it creates the conditions which make possible the doing of His will. Today the world is a unit of circumstance, and nothing less than some kind of supra-national government will do. The problem boils down to our need for an adequate international organization based on adequate international authority over all common judical, military, and economic functions.

The judicial authority must include effective instruments for dynamic and just change on the part of its several members.

---

[1] A convenient halfway measure might be the Swedish system which aims at the common good by a system of checks and balances between government ownership, co-operatives, and "free enterprise."

Effective international military authority would demand the total disarmament of all its members and the creation of an adequate international police force. Possibly Ely Culbertson's idea of a federal force, that is, one rationed proportionally from the different regions, interests, or races of the world, would be a good way of preventing a small clique from ruling a disarmed world by means of the international police force. It is well, in any case, to be aware of the danger and take proper precautions to have such a force as directly as possible responsible to the peoples of the world.

Effective economic authority would take in effective power over currency, raw materials, labor, migration, and all the internal decisions of the member states which vitally affect other states. This means, frankly, the cessation of sovereign nations. Naturally, nations will still be the dominant units of general government. We need effective internationalism, not cosmopolitan utopianism. The United World as one general unit may come some day, but we are far from ready for it at this time. The problem will, of course, be greatly eased as more and more states become fully socialist and democratic in the full meaning of these terms. The world government would then constitute the central planning board and executive office for the world. The enormous benefits of co-operation, in terms of the doing away with man's greatest social burden, our present divisive and excessive militarism, and the production instead almost entirely of positive economic goods, would make odious as a nightmare the old system of competition, conflict, and continuous destruction.

This is a view of the world for which we as Christians ought surely to work with all our powers. It means the cessation not only of divisive national sovereignty but also of imperialism. All imperialism must go as quickly as possible and be fulfilled in effective internationalism. The backwardness of some regions of the world is no excuse for continued domination and exploitation. Russia in one generation became a highly literate nation. Self-consciousness is rising all over the world and our global wars have, for some time now, produced basic revolutions in the outlook of perhaps all ruled peoples. All peoples are made by God, are ends of His creation, can contribute mightily to a rich new world, must be set free to develop their own genius, and must be given all the necessary resources to do so within a new world of responsibility on the part of all for the sake of all. We must under no circumstances give in to soft assurances of a "reformed" imperialism. The whole system is evil, prolongs dependency, and, in fact, perpetuates the very conditions which are used as an excuse for the rule of the strong over the weak.

Surely this does not mean, however, that we shall foist our own inadequate kind of democracy on all other peoples. We must start where they are and then help them to develop as quickly as possible toward democratic socialism. We do not know the future, but no outcome of the war, whether negotiated peace, a limited victory by either side, or even a complete victory by either side, can in the end stop the deeper forces of history.[2] Only spiritual and moral exhaustion and a resultant general decline of all civilization can stop the coming of social democracy and of world government. The masses are rising like sleeping giants, they organize and will increasingly control their own propaganda, and the very technological advance of the world of today and of tomorrow makes necessary such a full democracy and such an adequate world government.

In the new Christian society all racialism must also increasingly be eliminated. The causes of racialism naturally go ex-

[2] Cf. *The Christian Faith*, Chapter 3.

ceedingly deep and are enormously complicated, but two of its great causes are economic competition and all the frustrations which are due to it. This is true both within and among the nations. We want the non-white peoples to be our markets, not our competitors, and many of our rising problems are blamed on peoples different from us in order to take attention away from the real causes of our failures, or even to hide the real causes from ourselves. There are other factors for racialism— strangeness, ignorance, historic prejudice, ethnocentrism, cultural parochialism, etc.—but even though we need to work harder than ever in the realms of education and of moral motivation, we can change attitudes more radically by the constructive transformation of social and economic patterns than through mere exhortations or idealistic projects.

In the new world racialism must go. Christians surely should be aware of the fact that we may some day witness a race war on a world scale horrible beyond imagination and even the possible enslavement of the white man by the non-white. The time is surely short for us to repent on this score and yet we repent not. The day of doom may be nearer than we think. Shall we see it, or our children, or our children's children? If the fig tree ripens, what will be the harvest? Perhaps we shall pay in blood, sweat, and tears for all the evils under the sun which we have inflicted on our colored brothers, who before God are our equals. Surely their blood cries against us from the ground of all the earth. Have we at home, and in all human relations to the end of the earth, the power and the wisdom to apply radical Christianity to the race problem? Racialism is not a part of human nature but of social patterns and prejudice. Only a few years ago, as history goes, Russia treated the Jews as badly as any of the great nations in Europe, while

Germany treated them among the best. Today the situation is entirely reversed.

Finally Christianity must destroy war. War is rising against all men to devour them. War is the final incarnation in history of all its demonic forces. In our modern society there is never true and deep peace. There is always war whether overt or latent. The causes of war, too, are so deep and exceedingly complex that the more we have studied them the less we feel able to generalize about them. Those who have given much time and thought to the problem are wary of all easy solutions and sweeping generalizations. Yet two main causes are undeniably our system of economic conflict and the lack of any adequate international system to settle disputes and facilitate needed change. Out of these rise, to a great extent, nationalism, racialism, and all the other defensive rationalizations which unify one society against the other. The fact is that men's moral and spiritual vision, or their cultural and psychological progress, have not kept pace with their phenomenal technological progress.

It is easy to understand why the Orient should have been so comparatively peaceful over long epochs of time while the dynamic Occident should have had an almost continuous stream of wars. Our rate of extensive progress in terms of economic history has put an ever increasing strain on the widening and changing unities. It is folly not to think of civilizations based on slavery or serfs as forms of capitalism where the few control the main means of production and where increasing control of capital and labor means increasing wealth and prestige and, therefore, becomes a cause of conflict. World socialism is different in kind from any previous civilization and offers social and economic patterns which are in a qualitative way different from all previous systems and which are intrinsically conducive to co-operation in a revolutionary way. Christians must, therefore, work both for a transformation of our economic system, which amounts in fact to a radical revolution in our way of life and thinking, and also for the construction of an adequate international government with effective international authority.

Christianity is radically opposed to war because it is radically opposed both to the attitudes and to the system which produce war. Christianity radically rejects war. It is man's supreme denial of fellowship on the basis of *agape*. Christian pacifism, however, is powerless if it is merely a perfectionist movement for personal holiness. Christian pacifism cannot be a matter of perfectionist isolationism. It cannot be what Russell Stafford calls "the Christian Science of politics." As such it is neither deeply effective nor deeply Christian. Pacifism is Christian and effective only as a dramatic opposition to the radical causes of war and to the war itself as the final demonic crystallization of those causes. Pacifism must be a dramatic, constructive counter-proposal to the war system. The pacifism of radical Christianity confronts our whole actual system with the whole Gospel of Christ. Christians may differ as to their concrete actions during a war, but no radical Christian can deny the complete necessity of doing away with war. Christians at all times keep "the unity of the spirit in the bond of peace."

Never can a radical Christian participate in the hate and narrow nationalism of war. Every radical Christian works, rather, to do away with the causes of war, to heal the wounded in mind, heart, and body, and to produce those social, economic, and political patterns at home and in all the world which will be the constant occasion for a positive peace. Some of us believe very deeply, furthermore, that the Church should radically disassociate itself from all wars, become an intensive fellowship that can offer the world a new hope in deed as well as in theory, fight with its own weapons a victorious battle of the Holy Spirit, and be the Church of Christ throughout all times and seasons, not only in word but also in a living, world-transforming reality.

We are convinced that we must not personally, as far as we can help it, conform to the warring ways of the world, but must become transformed by the renewing of our minds in the radical Christian faith of the Gospel. We are all, of course, caught up in an inescapable situation, but how long that situation remains in the history of the world depends critically upon what we who want to be Christians really believe and do. The deepest conflicts in man and among men can never be done away without the drastic surgery of God's love. Christian peacemaking gets at the source of the whole stream of conflicts, in persons, in families, among nations. Upon the basic platform of radical world-transformation in the light of God as *agape* all true Christians, whether pacifists or non-pacifists, must in any case agree. Our own consciences before God, as free as possible from all rationalization, can alone convict and convince us of the most effective ways and means to bring this about.

For the Christian who accepts his religion radically the first and primary front of battle is always the spiritual. He views all things in the light of God's gracious yet judging revelation in Jesus Christ. He knows that the evils of society are the objectification of man's sins and limitations. For this reason he is wise enough to understand that no change in externals, however drastic, can be enough. The source must itself be cured. But he knows also that man's creations in history react on him and on his children in such a crucial way that it is not enough merely to try to convert people. The modern age needs, hand in hand, a spiritual conversion as profound in head, hand, and heart as radical Christianity and a social transformation as revolutionary as the Christian ideal of society. With full stress on both, the Christian under God will bring about important and lasting change.

This generation has been witnessing the organizational spread and development of the Christian institution throughout the whole earth. The Christian Church has in its hands the key to the new world to whatever extent it is radically a Christian fellowship. True, foreign missions have been prostituted for limited purposes and much can be said of the failures of modern missionaries. Yet despite its failures this movement is a natural and inevitable expression of the Christian spirit without which it is no longer Christian. In every last corner of the world there exists Christian fellowship. Even if we should live for an epoch in comparatively tightly sealed regions of the world, that fellowship would reach through God in Christ across all closed boundaries.

It is a fellowship that no outside power can break. Upon its degree of genuineness depends heavily the future of the world. If the true seed of the Kingdom has been sown we shall, as Jesus predicts, sleep and rise night and day and see it spring up we know not how for the redemption of the whole world. The only world-wide organization with every tribe and tongue is the Christian Church. The outward means are now ready. Whenever, therefore, the Church becomes resolutely and radically itself, no evil power, however dire and deep in human history, shall be able to withstand it, for unto it is given once for all the keys of the Kingdom that without its inmost reality, the kind of fellowship which Christianity alone can give, no man should taste salvation.